# HAIKUS

BY LISA M. BOLT SIMONS

ILLUSTRATED BY KATHLEEN PETELINSEK

**The Child's World**

Published by The Child's World®
1980 Lookout Drive · Mankato, MN 56003-1705
800-599-READ · www.childsworld.com

ACKNOWLEDGMENTS
The Child's World®: Mary Berendes, Publishing Director
Red Line Editorial: Editorial direction
The Design Lab: Design and production

Photographs ©: Thinkstock, 6; Vitaly Ilyasov/Shutterstock
Images, 13; Shutterstock Images, 19

ISBN 9781631436956
LCCN 2014945307

Printed in the United States of America
Mankato, MN
November, 2014
PA02240

## About the Author

Lisa M. Bolt Simons is a writer and a teacher. She has published more than ten books for children. She has also been awarded grants and awards for her writing. Besides writing, teaching has been her passion for 20 years. She lives in Minnesota with her husband and boy/girl twin teenagers. Her Web site is *www.lisamboltsimons.com*.

## About the Illustrator

Kathleen Petelinsek is a graphic designer and illustrator. She has been designing and illustrating books for children for 20 years. She lives in Minnesota with her husband, two dogs, a cat, and three fancy chickens.

# TABLE OF CONTENTS

CHAPTER ONE

1

# What **Is** a Poem?

Have you ever said a nursery rhyme before? Or memorized the words to a song? Did you know you were memorizing a poem? Poems are a special kind of writing. People use poetry to share stories and ideas. We also use poetry to describe the world. Poems help us remember things. People use poems to share stories and history.

Several things make poems different than other writing. Poems often use lines instead of sentences. A line can be as short as one word. It is not always a complete thought.

first syllable

second syllable

third syllable

**po·e·try**

All poems have **rhythm**. This is the way the words sound together. All words are made up of **syllables**. These are the different sounds that make up a word. For example, *po-em* has two parts. These parts are syllables. The word *po-e-try* has three syllables. Part of a poem's rhythm comes from the way its syllables sound together.

Beat is a part of rhythm. Beat is created with **stressed** and unstressed syllables. *FLOW-er* has stress on the first syllable. The word *a-WAKE* has stress on the second syllable. In poetry the pattern of these stresses is called meter.

*Clap words as you say them to check how many syllables they have. Hip-po-pot-a-mus has five syllables!*

Poets also create rhythm by changing line length. They can repeat words. Sometimes they add extra pauses. Rhythm can make poetry sound like music. Some poems are even turned into songs.

Many poems rhyme. But they don't have to! There are many different kinds of poems. You can write a poem about anything you want.

# WHAT IS A HAIKU?

Haikus are short poems that have a certain pattern of syllables. The first haikus were written in Japan. In Japanese, the word *haiku* means "beginning verse."

Haikus have a few important rules. A haiku is a tercet. This means it has three lines. The most well-known thing about haikus is the number of syllables. The first line in a haiku has five syllables. The second line has seven syllables. The third line has five again. Haikus have 17 syllables total.

A haiku's subject is also very important. Most haikus are about nature. Haikus often describe two things that are different from each other, such as a maple tree and a bonfire. These different things

might share a common feature. Maple trees turn orange in the fall. A bonfire is also orange. Haiku writers try to make readers think about the different things in new ways. Writers use the five senses to help their haikus come to life.

Matsuo Basho was a Japanese haiku poet in the 1600s. He wrote that haikus should be about what is happening right now. This means haikus are usually written in present tense. For example, a poet would write "sings" or "singing" instead of "sang."

Haikus are short. Writers must choose their words carefully. Haiku poets usually try not to use many descriptive words. Poets also avoid conjunctions. Conjunctions are connecting words like *and* or *but*. But it's OK to break rules when writing a haiku.

Flying, then it lands
the red insect with black spots
between the glass panes.

**?**

Can you guess what insect the poet is writing about in this haiku?
What words in the haiku helped you figure out the insect is a ladybug?

# Nature and Seasons

Like many poems, haikus use images. Images are what readers see inside their heads. Images help readers think about a poem. The words a poet chooses help create images. Because haikus are short, images are very important. They help the reader infer, or guess, what is not written by the poet.

Haikus are usually about nature. They can be about landscapes or animals. They can be about flowers or plants. Nature haikus use images from the environment.

*Details are the parts of something that make it different from others like it. This is especially important in short haikus. A detail for fall could be a squirrel burying nuts.*

Word choice is important in haikus. It is better to use specific words than general words. This means instead of writing "bird," write "bluebird" or "robin." Instead of just writing "moon," add "crescent" or "full."

Haikus are often written about the four seasons. Haiku poets write about spring, summer, fall, and winter.

There isn't room for many details in a haiku. Usually, writers give specific word clues. These are hints about what season the writer is talking about. Then the reader can guess the season. Clues could also be about other images in a haiku. Instead of writing "cardinal," the poet could write "a red bird with a Mohawk." A crescent moon could be described as an orange slice in the sky.

Sweet mint and candy
mixed in ice cream chills my tongue,
while snow blankets grass.

**?**

What is the clue that it's winter? What else is happening in this haiku?

CHAPTER THREE

3

# Comparisons and Senses

Haikus often feature details using comparisons and senses. The things being compared can be very different. A haiku might say, "Air is hot soup on my skin." The reader guesses the weather is warm and humid.

A simile compares two things that are alike. The writer uses the words *like* or *as*. For example, "Your puffy white jacket looks like a marshmallow" is a simile. "My brother jumps on the trampoline as high as a kangaroo" is another simile.

Haikus usually use **metaphors** instead of similes. A metaphor compares two things that are alike. But *like* or *as* is not written. "Your jacket is a marshmallow" is a metaphor. "My brother is a kangaroo on the trampoline" is another metaphor. Metaphors help make haikus interesting for readers.

Senses also help make a haiku interesting to a reader. The five senses are sight, sound, taste, touch, and smell. Using words that relate to these senses gives readers clues about a haiku's subject. Haikus sometimes describe senses in surprising ways. People probably don't think of hot soup when they feel the summer air. Using this comparison helps readers think about summer in a new way.

*The wind through the trees makes different sounds in different seasons. Summer trees make a shushing sound. Autumn leaves make a crackling noise. What might winter trees sound like?*

The nighttime spring rain
plunges from blankets of clouds,
pricks forks in my skin.

**?**

Does this haiku use a metaphor or a simile? How
does the author feel about the spring rain?

# NOW IT'S YOUR TURN!

Haikus are short poems. With only 17 syllables, poets must choose their words carefully. Putting a haiku together can be like baking cookies with three ingredients. Only the right three ingredients will make delicious cookies. Now that you know what a haiku is, it's time to write your own!

FIVE SYLLABLES

SEVEN SYLLABLES

FIVE SYLLABLES

# TIPS FOR YOUNG POETS

1. Write a haiku every day for a month.

2. Learn the rules for two types of poems. Then use the rules you learned to write two poems about the same topic. How are your poems different?

3. Pick an everyday object, such as a food. Then describe it using all five senses. Pick one or two of these senses, and write a haiku.

4. Try writing poems that do not rhyme.

5. Watch and listen to the world around you. Make a list of the things you see and hear. Use this list to write a poem.

6. Think of something that happened to you today. Write a haiku about it in the present tense.

7. Read all kinds of poems and lots of them. The best way to learn about poetry is to read it!

8. Write haikus for all four seasons, and read them to an audience. Can they infer the season? Can they guess how you feel about the season?

# GLOSSARY

**infer (in-FUR):** To infer is to use facts and details to make a good guess about something. When you read a poem, you infer the poet's meaning.

**metaphors (MET-uh-forz):** Metaphors compare two things that share a similar feature without using the words *like* or *as*. "The sun was a red dragon" and "the moon was an orange" are examples of metaphors.

**rhythm (RITH-uhm):** Rhythm is a repeating pattern of sounds in poetry. Music also has rhythm.

**simile (SIM-uh-lee):** A simile compares two things that share a similar feature, using the words *like* or *as*. "He was as fast as a rocket" is an example of a simile.

**stressed (STREST):** A word or syllable is stressed when it is said a bit stronger or louder than another word or syllable. The first syllable is stressed in *OR-ange*.

**syllables (SIL-uh-buhlz):** Syllables are units of sounds in a word. You can tell how many syllables are in a word by clapping your hands as you say the word.

**tercet (TER-set):** A tercet is a poem with three lines. A haiku is an example of a tercet.

# TO LEARN MORE

## BOOKS

Bodden, Valerie. *Poetry Basics: Haiku.* Mankato, MN: The Creative Company, 2011.

Higgins, Nadia. *Henry and Hala Build a Haiku.* Chicago: Norwood House Press, 2011.

Rosen, Michael J. *The Hound Dog's Haiku: And Other Poems for Dog Lovers.* Somerville, MA: Candlewick Press, 2011.

## ON THE WEB

Visit our Web site for lots of links about haikus:
www.childsworld.com/links

*Note to Parents, Teachers, and Librarians: We routinely check our Web links to make sure they're safe, active sites—so encourage your readers to check them out!*

# INDEX